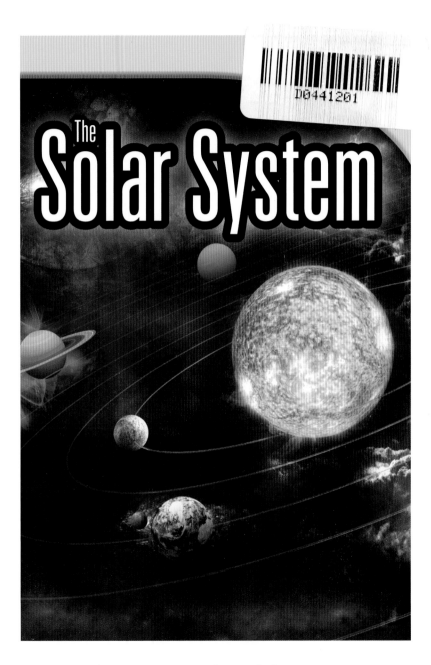

The Solar System

Kenneth Walsh

Consultant

Timothy Rasinski, Ph.D.
Kent State University

Publishing Credits

Dona Herweck Rice, *Editor-in-Chief*
Robin Erickson, *Production Director*
Lee Aucoin, *Creative Director*
Conni Medina, M.A.Ed., *Editorial Director*
Jamey Acosta, *Editor*
Stephanie Reid, *Photo Editor*
Rachelle Cracchiolo, M.S.Ed., *Publisher*

Image Credits
Cover adventtr/iStockphoto; p.4 avian/Shutterstock; p.5 Hogie/Shutterstock; p.6-7 xJJx/Shutterstock;
p.8 NASA/European Space Agency; p.9 Max Dannenbaum/GettyImages; p.10 NASA/JPL; p.11 middle:
Xirurg/iStockphoto; p.11 bottom: Clara/Shutterstock; p.12 Plutonius 3d/Shutterstock; p.13 NASA/JPL;
p.14 NASA; p.15 top: NASA/JPL/Malin Space Science Systems; p.15 left: NASA/JPL; p.16 NASA/JPL; p. 15
right: Malin Space Science Systems; p.17 NASA/Jet Propulsion Laboratory; p.18 NASA/Erich Karkoschka,
University of Arizona; p.19 top: JCEIv/Shutterstock; p.19 bottom: NASA/Space Telescope Science Institute;
p.21 MichaelTaylor/Shutterstock; p.23 right: LKPalmer-Illustration; p.23 left: NASA; p.24 NASA/JPL-Caltech;
p.25 Leagam/Shutterstock; p.26 STEVECOLEccs/Shutterstock; p.27 top: Binkski/Shutterstock; p27 bottom:
Witold Kaszkin/Shutterstock; p.28 NASA/JPL; back cover NASA/JPL; background untung/Shutterstock

Based on writing from *TIME For Kids*.

Teacher Created Materials

5301 Oceanus Drive
Huntington Beach, CA 92649-1030
http://www.tcmpub.com
ISBN 978-1-4333-3633-1
© 2012 Teacher Created Materials, Inc.
Reprinted 2013

Table of Contents

Moving Around the Sun

Think of yourself standing on the ground. The ground is on Earth, and Earth is moving in space around the **sun**.

The sun is the center of our **solar system**. You and everything else on Earth are moving in **orbit** around it.

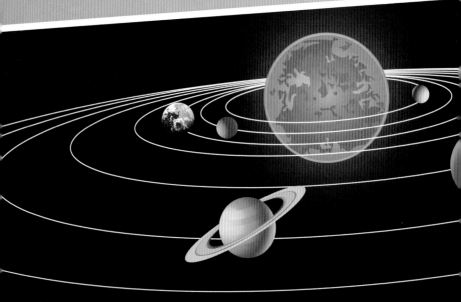

Orbiting the Sun

An orbit is the path a planet follows when it moves around the sun. Each planet has a different orbit, and each orbit takes a different amount of time to complete. To read more about orbits, turn to page 22.

One Sun

The center of our solar system is the sun. *Solar* means sun.

The sun is very large. It is hard to imagine its size. Can you imagine the size of Earth? As big as Earth is, the sun is a million times bigger!

From Earth, the sun looks like a big, yellow ball. But it is not really like a ball. It is made of gases and metals. It is also very hot. Nothing can live on the sun. But it is a good thing the sun is so hot. The sun's heat makes Earth warm enough for people to live.

The North star is just one of many stars shining brightly over Earth.

The sun is actually a star, just like the other stars in the night sky. But it is much nearer to Earth than the other stars are.

The Eight Planets

Mars

Earth

Jupiter

Saturn

Venus

Mercury

Earth is just one **planet** that moves around the sun. There are eight planets in all. The closest planet to the sun is Mercury. Then come Venus, Earth, Mars, Jupiter, Saturn, Uranus, and Neptune.

Neptune

Uranus

Planet Names

All of the planets except Earth are named for characters in mythology. For example, Mars is the Roman god of war, and Venus is the Roman goddess of love and beauty. Earth's name comes from the ancient Greek, German, and English words for land.

Venus

Mars

Some scientists think that there may be other planets, but they do not know for sure.

There are special things about each planet that make it different from the others. Here are some interesting facts:

Mercury

Mercury seems to be the fastest planet because its orbit is so small.

Venus has been nicknamed the Morning and Evening Star.

Venus is the brightest planet in the sky.

Earth

Earth is the only planet in our solar system known to have life.

Mars

Moon

Earth

Jupiter

Mars Orbiter Camera

This photo of Earth, Earth's moon, and Jupiter was taken from Mars with the Mars Orbiter Camera.

Mars has very long, cold winters.

At its largest, the Great Red Spot on Jupiter is as big as three Earths!

Jupiter

The largest planet is Jupiter.

Saturn

Saturn's Rings

Galileo Galilei discovered Saturn's rings in 1610. Each ring moves around the planet at a different speed.

Rings made of rocks, gases, and ice surround Saturn.

Uranus

For a long time, people thought Uranus was a star.

Neptune

windstorms

Neptune has the fastest and strongest winds of any planet.

The planets may be different, but they have things in common, too. For example, most planets have moons. Some planets have many moons! This chart shows how many moons each planet has.

Planet Name	Number of Moons
Mercury	0
Venus	0
Earth	1
Mars	1
Jupiter	16
Saturn	18+
Uranus	15
Neptune	8

Moons

Moons are bodies that orbit planets. They are also called *satellites*. Saturn has 18 moons for sure, but we believe it has many more than that. Other planets may also have more moons. The more we are able to travel into space, the more we can discover and know.

Pluto

Pluto was once the ninth planet in our solar system. It was once thought to be a planet, but now it is called a *dwarf planet*. Pluto still moves around the sun.

Orbits and Rotations

Something else planets have in common is the way they move. All planets orbit around the sun. But each planet's orbit is different.

One orbit is the same as one year for that planet. Mercury has the shortest orbit. Its year is just one-fourth of Earth's year. Neptune's orbit is the longest, because it has the farthest distance to travel.

Each planet also spins around its own **axis** as it moves in orbit. One full spin is called a **rotation**. A rotation takes one day. On Earth, a day is 24 hours. Jupiter spins so fast that its day is less than 10 hours!

Axis Rotation

An axis is an imaginary pole running through the center of a planet. Imagine you have a ball with a stick through its center. If you hold the stick above and below the ball and spin the ball once around, it will make a rotation, just like a planet does.

Asteroids

Planets are not the only things that move around the sun. **Asteroids** do, too, but they are very small compared to planets. Even if you put all the asteroids in the solar system together, they would be much smaller than Earth's moon.

Asteroids

Asteroids are rocky, planet-like bodies that orbit the sun. Many asteroids travel together in the **asteroid belt** between Mars and Jupiter.

The best way to see an asteroid is in the night sky when it crosses Earth's orbit. It looks like a streak of light. We call this a **meteor**.

Next time you look up into the sky, think about everything that is out there. Now you know that Earth is just one part of this big, big solar system!

Glossary

asteroid—a small, rocky, planet-like body that orbits the sun

asteroid belt—an area between Mars and Jupiter in which many asteroids orbit the sun together

axis—the imaginary line through the center of a planet around which it rotates

meteor—a stone that falls from space towards Earth

orbit—the path a planet follows when it moves around the sun

planet—a large body in space that orbits a star

rotation—the spinning of a planet around its own axis

solar system—a group of planets and other heavenly bodies that move around a central sun

sun—the large and bright star at the center of our solar system